LIVING WATER

A LENTEN RETREAT GUIDE ON CHRIST'S ENCOUNTER WITH THE SAMARITAN WOMAN

FR. JOHN BARTUNEK, LC, STHD

ISBN-13: 9781793953414

This booklet is a part of RCSpirituality's *Retreat Guide* service, which includes free online videos and audio tracks available at **RCSpirituality.org**.

INTRODUCTION

Living Water

RETREAT OVERVIEW

Lent—the forty-day period of spiritual preparation for the most significant days of the Church's year: Holy Thursday, Good Friday, and Easter Sunday—is one of the oldest liturgical periods in the history of Christianity. Although its current form came about officially only in the fourth century, its special liturgical character was lived even earlier, throughout the era of Roman persecution.

For this reason, the Gospel passages that we proclaim at Mass each year on the Sundays of Lent also have a long history, especially the passages for the first year in the three-year cycle of Sunday readings. In fact, those passages have so long been part of the Lenten season that pastors always have the option of using them every year, not just once every three years.

This ancient tradition chooses as the Gospel passage for the Third Sunday of Lent the mysterious encounter between Jesus and the Samaritan woman. It takes place while Jesus is resting alone near Jacob's Well and his disciples have gone into town to get some supplies before continuing their journey. That encounter is the subject of this Retreat Guide.

o   The First Meditation will explore what this encounter reveals about Jesus himself.

o   The Second Meditation will explore what it reveals about us.

o   And the Conference will get practical by digging into what "doing God's will" really means and why Jesus puts so much importance on it.

Let's begin by quieting our hearts and minds and turning our attention to the Lord, who never stops paying attention to us. Let's ask him for all the graces we need, and most especially, for the grace to taste the living water that flows out of this encounter—and every encounter—with Jesus Christ.

NOTES

FIRST MEDITATION
Jesus Shows Us His Cards

INTRODUCTION

This encounter reveals at least three things about Jesus. We probably already know these things, at least as facts. But these characteristics of our Lord are part of God revealing who he is, and if we dig more deeply into them and give ourselves a chance to contemplate them, they can renew our relationship with God and continue to enrich our spiritual lives.

FULLY HUMAN

The first thing this encounter reveals about Jesus is so obvious we may overlook it. In John 4:6–7, St. John tells us the following:

Jesus, tired from his journey, sat down there at the well. It was about noon. A woman of Samaria came to draw water. Jesus said to her, "Give me a drink."

We can picture the scene. Jesus and his disciples have been walking the long road from Judea back to Galilee. It was hot and dusty traveling. The disciples have gone into Sychar to do a little shopping, and Jesus stays outside the town by Jacob's well. He is tired, exhausted, beat. He is thirsty. He is probably hungry too. And this woman who comes to draw water from the well (remember, she had no indoor plumbing—you had to go all the way to the town well to get your water) has a bucket (we find out later in the passage that Jesus had no bucket, nothing he could use to get some water). So he asks her for a drink.

Jesus is tired; Jesus is thirsty ... Jesus is fully human! Jesus, the Son of God, the Second Person of the Blessed Trinity, the incarnate Word of God, is tired and thirsty. He has to stop and rest. He has to ask someone for a drink.

Plenty of non-Christian religions have myths and traditions about various divinities or semi-divinities that take *human form* for one reason or another. But Jesus goes way beyond that. First of all, Jesus is God, not just one supposed god among a pantheon of flawed divinities—like Zeus or Apollo or Shiva—but the actual Creator of the universe, eternal and omnipotent in his divine nature. And second, when he decides to come and redeem the human race from sin and offer us everlasting salvation, he does so by *entering fully into our human reality*. He wants to be close to us. He wants us to know that *nothing* we suffer or experience is foreign or inconsequential to him. To save us and share his divine life with us, Jesus becomes one of us, fully, completely, marvelously. As the Letter to the Hebrews puts it:

> ... [T]herefore, he had to become like his brothers in every way, that he might be a merciful and faithful high priest before God to expiate the sins of the people. Because he himself was tested through what he suffered, he is able to help those who are being tested.

> —Hebrews 2:17–18

As Christians, if we really want to keep deepening our friendship with Jesus, we have to pause at this fact, a fact we have heard so many times. We have to contemplate it and keep it in mind. We have to ask the Lord, "Jesus, why did you save us this way? What do you want to say to me by becoming just like me, getting tired and thirsty and worn out?"

The second thing this encounter reveals about Jesus is also obvious: he is not only truly human, but he is also truly God—"true God and true man" as we say every Sunday when we pray the Creed.

This comes across in various places during Jesus's conversation with the Samaritan woman. In the first place, Jesus claims to be able to give "the gift of God," which he describes as the "living water" that will never run dry and will lead to everlasting life. Here are our Lord's own words:

> If you knew the gift of God and who is saying to you, "Give me a drink," you would have asked him and he would have given you living water … Everyone who drinks this water will be thirsty again; but whoever drinks the water I shall give will never thirst; the water I shall give will become in him a spring of water welling up to eternal life.
>
> —John 4:11, 13–14

These are some of the many "I statements" that Jesus makes throughout the Gospel of John. In these statements he makes claims that only God could fulfill, but he makes them about himself. He identifies himself with God—in this case, with the one who alone can give the gift of eternal life.

Later in the conversation, he makes another "I statement" in reference to the figure of the Messiah, the promised Savior spoken about in the Old Testament prophecies. Here is how St. John records the last snippet of the exchange:

> The woman said to him, "I know that the Messiah is coming, the one called the Anointed; when he comes, he will tell us everything." Jesus said to her, "I am he, the one who is speaking with you."
>
> —John 4:25–26

The combination of these two sets of "I statements" leaves no room for doubt: Jesus is God, humanity's one Lord and Savior—or else he is a liar, or a lunatic, or a liar *and* a lunatic.

FULLY INVOLVED

To prove to this woman that what he says is true, that he is the divine Savior, Jesus shows that he knows all about her—he reveals knowledge that, naturally speaking, he could never know: knowledge about this woman's present circumstances, and her past life. And this shows us the third thing this encounter reveals about Jesus.

It turns out that this woman is currently living with a man who is not her husband, and that she has already gone through five husbands. Jesus, a complete stranger, could have no way of knowing those things about her. But he does know them. And that, for this woman, is a game changer. She begins to believe that he truly might be what he claims to be, the divine Messiah, and she is so stunned and excited that she leaves her water jar right there at the well and rushes back into town to tell everyone about her discovery. St. John tells us:

> The woman left her water jar and went into the town and said to the people, "Come see a man who

told me everything I have done. Could he possibly be the Messiah?" … Many of the Samaritans of that town began to believe in him because of the word of the woman who testified, "He told me everything I have done."

—John 4:28, 39

But it must have been more than just Jesus's supernatural knowledge that moves this woman's heart and makes her into one of the first Christian missionaries. It is the entire encounter. This woman is considered a sinner and an outcast. Living with someone outside of wedlock after suffering a whole string of failed marriages … There is a reason she comes to the well in heat of the day all by herself, instead of coming earlier when all the women of the town would have been drawing their water together. She has been ostracized. She has lost her status. Her fellow Samaritans treat her with contempt and disdain.

But then this man, not even a Samaritan, claims to be the Messiah, the most exalted figure in Israel's entire history, proves his claim by showing supernatural knowledge, and treats her—an outcast—with dignity, respect, and generosity.

That's Jesus. True God and true man, Jesus cares about every single one of us. He reaches out to us, engages us in a conversation that becomes a relationship, and changes the direction of our lives, just as he did with the Samaritan woman. In Jesus's time, men didn't talk to women in public like this. Jews didn't talk to Samaritans like this. Rabbis didn't talk to notorious sinners like this. And yet, here Jesus is, breaking down all those social and cultural barriers in order to bring living water into this person's heart, which is dying of thirst.

JESUS MEETS US AT OUR WELL

Jesus wants to be involved in our lives. He truly cares. He is a *present* God who brings grace and redemption into our lives wherever we find ourselves. This is how he worked the first time we encountered him, and it is how he continues to work in the today of our lives, and how he will continue to work until our earthly journey is over and he takes us home.

Jesus is fully human. Jesus is the divine Messiah. Jesus wants to be involved in our lives, right where we are. These are three things this encounter reveals about our Lord. They are not new facts for us, perhaps, but they can strike us in a new way, and so renew our friendship with God, if we let them. Let's take some time now, in the quiet of our hearts, to do exactly that. The following questions and quotations may help your meditation.

QUESTIONS FOR PERSONAL REFLECTION/GROUP DISCUSSION

1. What does it mean to me that Jesus became fully human, that God became man in order to bring his saving grace into my life?

2. How would I answer the question: "Why did Jesus decide to redeem us by becoming one of us?"

3. How is God wanting to be involved in my life right now? How am I responding to his invitations?

QUOTATIONS TO HELP YOUR PRAYER

❝What does it mean then, for the pious Israelite, to seek the face of God, while recognizing that there can be no image of Him? The question is important: on the one hand, it is said that God cannot be reduced to an object, to a simple image, nor can anything be put in the place of God; on the other, however, it is affirmed that He has a face, that is, He is a "You" that can enter into a relationship, who isn't closed in his Heavens looking down upon humanity. God is certainly above all things, but he turns to us, hears us, sees and speaks, makes covenants, is capable of love. The history of salvation is history of God with humanity, it is the history of this relationship of God who progressively reveals himself to man, letting him see his face.

—General Audience, 16 January 2013
POPE BENEDICT XVI

❝God did not wait for everyone to go to Him, but it was He who moved toward us, without calculating, without measure. God is like this: He always takes the first step, He moves towards us… God came out himself to come among us, he has placed his tent among us to bring us God's mercy that saves and gives hope. We, too, if we want to follow Him and stay with Him, must not be content with staying in the enclosure of the ninety-nine sheep, we must "come out", to seek out with Him the lost sheep, the farthest. Mark this well: to come out of ourselves, like Jesus, like God came out of Himself in Jesus and Jesus came out of himself for all of us.

—General Audience, 27 March 2013
POPE FRANCIS

Jesus is God-with-us, Emmanuel. The great mystery of God becoming human is God's desire to be loved by us. By becoming a vulnerable child, completely dependent on human care, God wants to take away all distance between the human and the divine.[1]

—Henri Nouwen

NOTES

1   http://henrinouwen.org/meditation/gods-powerlessness/ (accessed 27 May 2018)

SECOND MEDITATION

Jesus Shows Us Our Cards

INTRODUCTION

This encounter doesn't just reveal things about Jesus; it also reveals things about us—at least three things worth reflecting on.

OUR THIRST

First, it reminds us that we too are thirsty. Listen to how the Samaritan woman responds when Jesus tells her about the living water, the water that only he can give, the water that alone will truly quench our thirst.

> Jesus answered and said to her, "Everyone who drinks this water will be thirsty again; but whoever drinks the water I shall give will never thirst; the water I shall give will become in him a spring of water welling up to eternal life." The woman said to him, "Sir, give me this water, so that I may not be thirsty or have to keep coming here to draw water."
>
> —John 4:13–15

Jesus is talking about the gift of the Holy Spirit, as St. John explains later, in Chapter 7 of his Gospel:

> On the last and greatest day of the feast, Jesus stood up and exclaimed, "Let anyone who thirsts come to me and drink. Whoever believes in me, as scripture says: 'Rivers of living water will flow from within him.'" He said this in reference to the Spirit that those who came to believe in him were to receive.
>
> —John 7:37–39

The Samaritan woman probably doesn't understand this yet. She is just tired of having to come all the way to the well every day to fill up her bucket and keep enough water in the house. She needs water—can't live without it, in fact. But it's not easy to keep a steady supply at hand. It takes a lot of work. Jesus's reference to living water sparks a hope that there may be another way.

THE HUMAN PREDICAMENT

Her predicament is our predicament. We are created with a thirst for meaning, purpose, and happiness. But as hard as we work to quench that thirst, no merely earthly pleasure, accomplishment, or relationship is enough to satisfy it. So we keep going back to the same wells, only to relieve our thirst temporarily; then we have to go back again. As human beings in a fallen world, we are unable to provide for ourselves what we most need: lasting satisfaction and meaning. We are thirsty—profoundly, existentially thirsty.

This predicament drives the many philosophies and religions of human history. Each one of them strives to answer our most fundamental, existential question: Where can we find the meaning and satisfaction we long for? What truly is the meaning of life?

Our thirst for meaning shines through in this passage. It's good for us to recognize this desire deep within us, to name it, to feel it, and to bring it to the Lord in prayer, just as the Samaritan woman did. If we ignore it or minimize it or consistently distract ourselves from it, we stifle spiritual progress.

OUR TROUBLE

The second thing this passage reveals about us is something Jesus himself mentions specifically later on, during the Last Supper. He tells his apostles: "In the world you will have trouble …" (John 16:33)

Think about the trouble this woman has had. She has been married five times. We don't know the details, but clearly those relationships made her suffer, over and over again. And now she is living with a man out of wedlock, which relegates her to outcast status. Like a leper, her neighbors avoid and stigmatize her, so much, in fact, that she has to come to the village well all by herself, when no one else will be there.

It is safe to say that life for the Samaritan woman probably feels more like a burden than a joy, at least most of the time. Regardless of how much or how little her own bad decisions have contributed to her situation, she is experiencing the trouble that comes from having a fallen human nature and living in a fallen world. And we share that same nature and live in that same world. This is why Jesus warns us: "In the world, you will have trouble…"

Often we forget this. Often we think that we could experience heaven on earth, getting rid of all our troubles, if only we could make a few adjustments in our relationships, our bank account, or our schedules. But nothing we do can change the fallen nature of this world—we can't turn it into heaven. And the more we learn to accept that, and to adjust our expectations accordingly, the more room God will have to continue working the miracle of redemption in our souls.

OUR TRANSFORMATION

The third thing this encounter reveals about us is that our lives truly can be different with Jesus. Although the world around us remains fallen, and we have to keep struggling with our own fallen nature, even so, God's grace truly does transform us and give us new life. The living water that Jesus promises is real.

We see it in the Samaritan woman's response to her conversation with Jesus. She rushes back to the town, filled with awe and energy. She discovers that she is known and loved, at least by Jesus, in spite of how the rest of the world may see her. She discovers that the promises of God are not just legend and myth, but reality—the Messiah is not a dream, but a real person.

Most of us have had this kind of experience at some point, an experience in which God touched us and changed us, changed the direction of our lives. But it doesn't end there. It just begins there. With God, there is always more to discover. And the more we encounter Jesus, the more he transforms us. He is not finished with us yet. He truly can make a difference in our lives, not just yesterday, but today as well, and tomorrow, and every single day of our lives.

This passage reminds us of that, and the Church never stops inviting us to believe in it, and to keep making room for Jesus so that the transformation continues. That's why this Gospel encounter has always had such a special place in the liturgy of Lent, because making more room for Jesus in our lives and in the lives of others, encountering him afresh, is what Lent and Holy Week are all about.

In the conference we will dig a little more deeply into how discovering and embracing God's will is one way Jesus satisfies our spiritual thirst. But for now, let's take some time, in the quiet of our hearts, to remember how we are in God's eyes: thirsty and troubled, but being transformed. The following questions and quotations may help your meditation.

QUESTIONS FOR PERSONAL REFLECTION/GROUP DISCUSSION

1. When do I experience the deep thirst for meaning and fulfillment that God has built into my human nature? How do I usually respond when I feel that thirst most intensely? What might Jesus have to say about that?

2. What types of things tend to cause me "trouble" in the sense that Jesus meant when he said, "In the world you will have trouble"? How do I usually respond when trouble presses upon me? What might Jesus have to say about that?

3. What difference has Jesus made in my life? What difference do I hope he will make in the near future? Speak to the Lord about your needs and his desires.

QUOTATIONS TO HELP YOUR PRAYER

Two evils my people have done:
they have forsaken me, the source of living waters;
They have dug themselves cisterns,
broken cisterns that cannot hold water.

—Jeremiah 2:13; 17:7–8
NABRE

❝...Blessed are those who trust in the LORD;
the LORD will be their trust.
They are like a tree planted beside the waters
that stretches out its roots to the stream:
It does not fear heat when it comes,
its leaves stay green;
In the year of drought it shows no distress,
but still produces fruit.

—Jeremiah 17:7–8
NABRE

❝On the last and greatest day of the feast, Jesus stood up
and exclaimed, "Let anyone who thirsts come to me
and drink. Whoever believes in me, as scripture says:
'Rivers of living water will flow from within him.' " He
said this in reference to the Spirit that those who came
to believe in him were to receive.

—John 7:37–39
NABRE

NOTES

CONFERENCE

What Is "God's Will"?

INTRODUCTION

When Jesus's disciples finish running errands in town and come back to Jacob's Well, after they recover from their surprise at Jesus talking alone with a Samaritan woman, they offer him some lunch. Here's how St. John (who was actually there) describes the exchange:

Meanwhile, the disciples urged him, "Rabbi, eat." But he said to them,"I have food to eat of which you do not know." So the disciples said to one another, "Could someone have brought him something to eat?" Jesus said to them,"My food is to do the will of the one who sent me and to finish his work."

—John 4:31–34

Jesus's food, so he tells his disciples, is "to do the will of the one who sent me, and to finish his work." Food is something we need, something we long for and hunger for, something that nourishes us and without which we simply cannot grow and flourish and become what we are created to be. That's what food is. And Jesus says that his food is to do his Father's will.

CHRIST'S DEEPEST DESIRE

Think about that for a moment. Think about how powerful that statement is. For Jesus, his very life, his most fundamental desire, is to do his Father's will. That's what he lives from; that's what nourishes him; that's what satisfies him.

It would be a powerful statement in itself, but it becomes even more powerful in the context of the rest of St. John's

Gospel. Because, in fact, this is only one of many, many, many times when Jesus expresses how absolutely central his Father's will is to his whole existence and mission. Here are just a few other examples.

Jesus answered and said to them, "Amen, amen, I say to you, a son cannot do anything on his own, but only what he sees his father doing; for what he does, his son will do also."

—John 5:19

I cannot do anything on my own; I judge as I hear, and my judgment is just, because I do not seek my own will but the will of the one who sent me.

—John 5:30

… I do nothing on my own, but I say only what the Father taught me.

—John 8:28

OUR SOURCE OF MEANING

So this is how Jesus lives—doing the will of his Father, staying united to his Father through obedience to his Father's will. His Father's will is the anchor of Jesus's life, his beacon, his compass. And when Jesus calls each one of us to be his followers, he calls us to have the same compass. Discovering and embracing God's will for our lives is how we grow in our friendship with Christ and help build his Kingdom on earth. It's the path to holiness. It's the source of the only meaning that will truly fulfill us.

Jesus makes this clear many times.

In his Sermon on the Mount, he puts it like this:

*Not everyone who says to me, "Lord, Lord," will enter the kingdom of heaven, but only the one who does the will of my Father in heaven.

—Matthew 7:21

In response to one listener who compliments him by saying, "Blessed is the womb that carried you and the breasts at which you nursed," he puts it like this:

*Rather, blessed are those who hear the word of God and observe it.

—Luke 11:27–28

In other words, true blessedness, true happiness, comes from discovering and fulfilling God's will for our lives.

This lesson is so central to Jesus's doctrine that he built it in to the fundamental prayer of Christianity, the Our Father. Every time we pray the Lord's Prayer, we say: "Thy Kingdom come, thy will be done on earth as it is in heaven" (Matthew 6:10). In other words, we ask God to bring his kingdom of peace, justice, and redemption into the world, and God himself has linked the coming of that Kingdom to our acceptance of his will.

FOLLOWING THE BEST EXAMPLES

This wasn't just a prayer that Jesus taught us. It is also a prayer that he prayed, and that his mother prayed.

When the Archangel Gabriel came to Mary at the annunciation, her response is: "Behold, I am the handmaiden of the Lord. May it be done to me according to your word" (Luke 1:38). The Blessed Virgin Mary understood herself as being entirely available for God's will.

And when Jesus entered into his own agony in the Garden of Gethsemane, he prays a similar prayer, multiple times. St. Matthew records it like this: "My Father, it if is possible, let this cup pass from me; yet, not as I will, but as you will" (Matthew 26:39). In a moment of deep suffering, disorientation, and confusion, Jesus himself clings once again to his Father's will as the rudder that will steer him through the darkness.

Discovering and embracing God's will, clearly, should be at the center of our lives as disciples of Jesus Christ: if, as he told the Samaritan woman, that is *his* food, then it should be *our* food too.

WHAT DO WE MEAN BY "GOD'S WILL"?

But what exactly is "God's will"? What does "Thy will be done" really refer to? That's what I would like to reflect on in the rest of this conference.

At the most basic level, the words "God's will" refer to two things.

First, they refer to what God wants for us in general, over all. Why did God create us? What does he have in store for us? Where does he want us to go in life? What is the final destination he has in mind for us? The answers to those questions are the first level of "God's will."

And second, the phrase "God's will" refers to the path God opens up for us that will lead us to that destination, the steps we need to take to get there.

Let's begin with the first meaning: What does God have in mind as our final destination?

Jesus Christ, the Word of God who became man and dwelt among us, has made this very clear. He expressed it most succinctly, perhaps, during the conversation with the Pharisees in which he described himself as the good shepherd who lays down his life for his sheep. In that same discourse, he explains the goal of his mission on earth, and reveals what God wants for us, what God's will for us, over all, really is. He tells us:

A thief comes only to steal and slaughter and destroy; I came so that they might have life and have it more abundantly.

— John 10:10

A more abundant life, a fulfilling, flourishing life, a life overflowing with meaning, purpose, and satisfaction. That's what God wants for us.

Earlier in that same Gospel, St. John said the same thing in different words:

For God so loved the world that he gave his only Son, so that everyone who believes in him, might not perish, but might have eternal life. For God did not send his Son into the world to condemn the world, but that the world might be saved through him.

— John 3:16–17

Everlasting life, salvation—those are other terms referring to the "more abundant life" that Jesus came to give us. This is God's will for us.

Another word for this over-all meaning of God's will is, simply, happiness. And in this sense, God's will and our will are one and the same. What we want, ultimately, is happiness. We can't stop wanting it. We were created for it. And since God was the one who created us, it makes perfect sense that that's what he wants for us too. Here's how the Catechism expresses this, when commenting on the human person's natural desire for happiness:

> This desire is of divine origin. God has placed it in the human heart in order to draw man to the One who alone can fulfill it.
>
> —CCC, 1718

OUR PATH TO HAPPINESS

And that points us toward the second meaning of the phrase, "God's will." It not only refers to the *destination* that God desires for us—a more abundant life, everlasting life, salvation, beatitude—but it also refers to the *path* God provides to lead us there.

As human beings, we are unique among the creatures of this visible universe. We are not automatically driven towards our destination by instinct alone, as squirrels or spiders are. We have received the gift of free will, by which we can actually choose our own path towards the happiness that we desire.

This freedom is part of our being created in God's image. It enables us to become partners in the redemption of the world and in the building up of God's eternal Kingdom in ways that squirrels and spiders never could. But it also opens up the possibility of our making wrong choices as we travel life's journey, choices that may appear to lead us towards happiness, but actually take us down wrong paths that lead only to frustration and misery. And the presence of evil in the world at times makes those wrong paths attractive to our fallen, wounded human nature.

This is why we pray every day, "Thy Kingdom come, thy will be done on earth as it is in heaven...do not lead us into temptation, but deliver us from evil." We ask the Lord to guide us along the true path, aware that we are vulnerable to temptation and in need of God's grace to follow what Jesus described as the "hard road" that leads us to our true destination:

> Enter by the narrow gate; for the gate is wide and the way is easy, that leads to destruction, and those who enter by it are many. For the gate is narrow and the way is hard, that leads to life, and those who find it are few.

> —Matthew 7:13–14

In this second sense of the phrase, the sense of the path that will lead to our true destination, God's will is revealed to us in five basic ways. When we freely choose to follow his will along life's journey, our relationship with him grows because we exercise our trust in his goodness and wisdom, and trust is always the currency of intimacy.

GOD'S WILL REVEALED IN THE COMMANDMENTS

The first way he reveals his will is through his commandments, as they have been given to us in the Bible and the teachings of the Church. This includes the Ten Commandments from the Old Testament, as well as Jesus's commandments and other teachings in the Gospels, like "love your neighbor as yourself" (Mark 12:31) and "love one another as I have loved you" (John 15:12). Even the beatitudes, though not expressed as commandments, contain concrete guidance about how to live life as it is meant to be lived.

GOD'S WILL IN OUR DAILY RESPONSIBILITIES

Second, we find God's will in the normal responsibilities of our daily life. This is also traditionally called the "duties of our state in life."

Jesus, Mary, and Joseph spent many years living a very normal life in Nazareth. They grew in holiness and gave glory to God by being honest and hardworking, by taking care of each other and of friends and family, and by contributing to the life of the synagogue and the town.

This is the day-to-day arena of God's will. He wants us to live our normal human responsibilities with love and virtue, and in doing so we help make the world a better place, as well as growing in integrity and depth as human beings, by advancing "in wisdom and age and favor before God and man," as St. Luke describes Jesus during his years growing up in Galilee (Luke 2:52).

GOD'S WILL IN THE VOICE OF CONSCIENCE

Third, God guides us along life's path through the voice of our conscience, which is able to apply universal moral principles to our particular situations. Here is how the Catechism describes our conscience, quoting the Second Vatican Council:

❝Deep within his conscience man discovers a law which he has not laid upon himself but which he must obey. Its voice, ever calling him to love and to do what is good and to avoid evil, sounds in his heart at the right moment. … For man has in his heart a law inscribed by God. … His conscience is man's most secret core and his sanctuary. There he is alone with God whose voice echoes in his depths.

—CCC, 1776

That interior voice, drawing us to do what is right and to avoid what is wrong, enlightening us in difficult moments, and instructing us after we have made our choices—that too is one way God reveals his will to each one of us.

Because of our fallen human nature, however, our conscience is not automatically infallible: it needs to be formed. We need to fill our minds with the truths of our faith and use our reason to understand them. This enables our conscience to function in a healthy way. It's not always easy, but it's always important.

GOD'S WILL IN LIFE'S PROVIDENTIAL CIRCUMSTANCES

Fourth, God's will is often revealed to us through the providential circumstances of our lives. God is guiding history, and even in its small events and happenings we can find his action and his voice, if we learn to watch and listen. Here is how the Catechism explains it:

❝The witness of Scripture is unanimous that the solicitude of divine providence is concrete and immediate; God cares for all, from the least things

to the great events of the world and its history...
Divine providence consists of the dispositions by
which God guides all his creatures with wisdom
and love to their ultimate end.

—CCC, 303, 322

This is why, for example, Jesus could draw spiritual lessons
from the way the flowers grow and the way a farmer tends
his crops. This is why the horrible crime of betraying,
condemning, and crucifying Jesus was transformed into
the true story of God's infinite love and omnipotent
goodness redeeming the fallen world.

GOD'S WILL IN PERSONALIZED INSPIRATIONS

Fifth, and finally, God also speaks to us through
personalized inspirations. These are interior motions or
words that we know do not come just from ourselves, and
that spur us on towards doing or saying things that help
us fulfill our mission in life. St. John Paul II, for example,
started the tradition of celebrating World Youth Day not
just because someone had a brilliant idea, but because
he felt God moving him to welcome that idea in the
depths of his heart.

CHRIST'S FOOD—OUR FOOD

God's will—this is our food, our nourishment. This is what
will help us grow and flourish and become all that we are
created to be in this life and in the next. Growth in friendship
with Christ requires that we, like Jesus himself, and like the
Blessed Virgin Mary, seek always to discover and embrace
God's will for our lives as he continues to reveal it through
the commandments, the responsibilities of our daily lives,

the voice of conscience, the providential circumstances around us, and the inspirations of the Holy Spirit. True friends share each other's deepest values and desires. Every time we choose to discover and embrace God's will, we are choosing to invest in our friendship with God.

Making God's will our top priority is how we truly "seek first the Kingdom of God and his righteousness." And if we do that, Jesus promised, everything else will work itself out (cf. Matthew 6:33).

Take some time now to prayerfully consider the personal questionnaire, which is designed to help you apply these general Christian truths to your particular situation.

PERSONAL QUESTIONNAIRE

1. Jesus explained that he hungered for the Father's will. What do I hunger for in the depths of my soul? What is my spiritual "food"?

2. How often do I think about discovering and embracing "God's will"? How central is that concept to my worldview?

3. How deeply do I believe that God truly wants me to have "a more abundant life"?

4. How well have I come to understand the teachings of the Bible and the Church about God's commandments? How fully do I understand what Christian behavior really looks like?

5. What are my main day-to-day responsibilities in the current season of my life? How aware am I that those responsibilities are an expression of God's will for me?

6. How well have I formed my conscience, through studying my faith, through making good use of the sacrament of confession, through getting good advice from mentors or spiritual directors, and through regular and personal prayer?

7. How easily can I recognize the voice of conscience when it speaks deep within my soul? How do I usually respond to that voice?

8. How firmly do I believe in the reality of God's providence, especially regarding the events and circumstances of my daily life that are outside my control? What kind of an effort do I make to try to discover God's hand at work in the difficulties and challenges that come my way?

9. When have I experienced a personalized inspiration from the Holy Spirit? How did I respond and what were the results?

10. Have I learned to distinguish the difference between real inspirations from the Holy Spirit and whims and daydreams that are mere distractions? What can I do to learn to distinguish them better?

NOTES

FURTHER READING

If you feel moved to continue reflecting and praying about this theme, you may find the following books helpful:

Introduction to the Devout Life
by St. Francis de Sales

Christian Self-Mastery
by Basil Maturin

In the School of the Holy Spirit
by Jacques Philippe

Discerning the Will of God
by Timothy Gallagher. OMV

God's Voice Within
by Mark Thibodeaux, SJ

EXPLORING MORE

Please visit our website, *RCSpirituality.org,* for more spiritual resources, and follow us on Facebook for regular updates: *facebook.com/RCSpirituality.*

If you would like to support and sponsor a Retreat Guide, please consider making a donation at RCSpirituality.org.

Retreat Guides are a service of Regnum Christi.
RegnumChristi.org

Produced by Coronation Media.
CoronationMedia.com

Developed & Self-published by RCSpirituality.
RCSpirituality.org

Prep. for Total
Consecration to
O. Lady.
at
www.OurLady33.com

Printed in Great Britain
by Amazon

37923515R00033